For Tom M – J.A.

KINGFISHER
Kingfisher Publications Plc
New Penderel House
283–288 High Holborn
London WC1V 7HZ
www.kingfisherpub.com

First published in paperback by Kingfisher Publications Plc 2002
2 4 6 8 10 9 7 5 3 1
First published in hardback by Kingfisher Publications Plc 2000
2 4 6 8 10 9 7 5 3 1

1TR/1001/TWP/DIG(MAR)/150NYM

A CIP catalogue record for this book is available from
the British Library.

ISBN 0 7534 0669 1 (paperback)
ISBN 0 7534 0422 2 (hardback)

Editor: Katie Puckett
Series Designer: Jane Tassie

Printed in Singapore

Up the Garden Path

Are You a Spider?

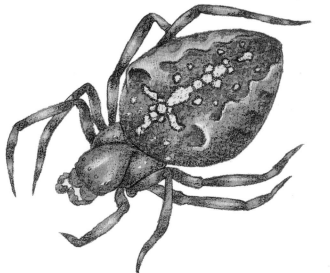

Judy Allen and Tudor Humphries

KING*f*ISHER

Are you a spider?
If you are, your mother
looks like this and
spins webs.

Your mother laid eggs
and wrapped them in a parcel
of silk. You were inside one of them.

When you break out of your egg,
you will find you have a lot of
brothers and sisters.

You are all small,
but you will all get bigger.

You look perfect.

You have a tiny waist and eight hairy legs.

You have two handy claws for pushing food into your mouth.

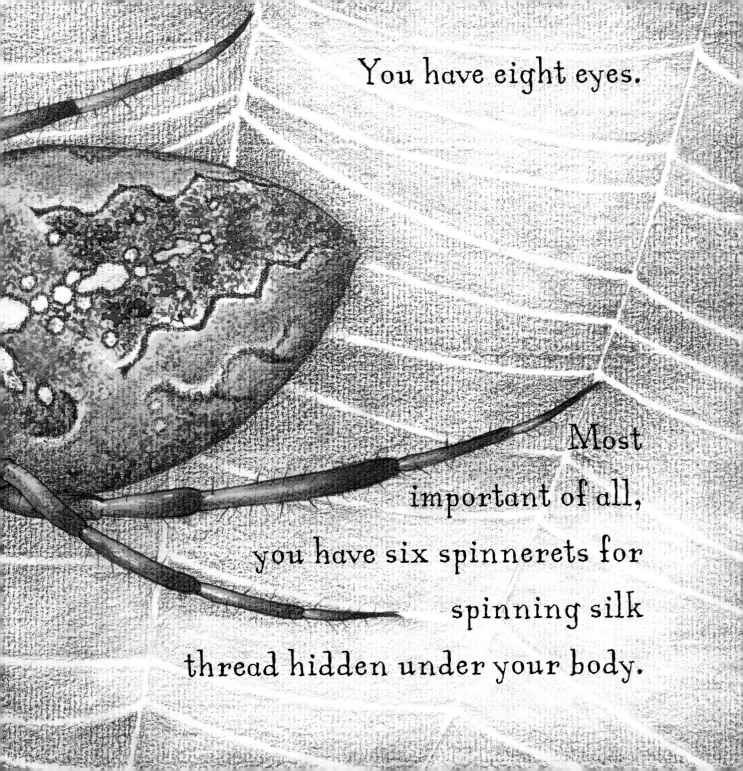

You have eight eyes.

Most
important of all,
you have six spinnerets for
spinning silk
thread hidden under your body.

Silk thread is the most
important thing in your life.

Begin to spin some at once.

You need it to help you move
away and start your own life.

Spin out the thread so it floats
in the air. With luck, a breeze
will catch it and carry
you away.

Or you could just walk.

Use your silk thread as a safety line when you walk.

If you fall, hang by your line
until you stop swinging.

Then climb back up it again.

Use your silk thread to build a web.

A web will catch flies,
and flies are good to eat.

Fix these threads first.
These threads must be
very strong.

This is hard work.

Fix these threads next.

These threads
must be very sticky.

This is even harder work.

Congratulations!
You have built a beautiful web.

When a fly flies
into your web, it will
stick there. Run and bite it.

Your bite will make
it go to sleep.

You can eat it now.

Or you can wrap it in silk thread and save it for later.

Watch out for birds.
Birds are dangerous.
Birds eat spiders.

Hide under a leaf.
That way the birds
won't see you.

Keep one foot on your web.
If the web shakes, you
will know you have
caught a fly.

Watch out for wasps.
Wasps are dangerous.
A wasp sting can
kill a spider.

If you catch a
wasp in your web,
don't try to eat it.
Try to cut it free.

Be sure to keep away from
the end that stings.

However, if you look
in a mirror and you
look something like this

or this

or this

or this

you are not a spider.

You are...

... a human child.

You do not have eight eyes or eight hairy legs.

You may have a tiny waist, but you definitely don't have spinnerets, and you can't spin silk thread.

Never mind, you will be able
to do a great many things spiders
can't do.

You must still be careful of wasps,
but you don't have to go to all the
bother of making a web.

Best of all, you will never,
ever, EVER have to wrap up
a fly and eat it.

Did You Know...

...spider-silk is very strong and elastic, and spinning it takes a lot of spider-energy – when a web is damaged a spider will often eat it before making a new one.

...there are more than 35,000 different kinds of spiders in the world.

...this is a garden spider, but other kinds include jumping spiders, trap-door spiders, tiny money spiders, water spiders, crab-spiders, tarantulas, wandering spiders, huntsman spiders, spitting spiders and tropical orb-web spiders whose webs are more than 2 metres wide.

...the smallest spiders are only about 1mm long, but the goliath tarantula has a leg span almost as wide as a dinner plate.